cooking the MEXICAN way

Spoonfuls of sour cream add just the right touch to *enchiladas con pollo*. (Recipe on page 22.)

cooking the
MEXICAN way

ROSA CORONADO

easy menu *ethnic* **cookbooks**

Lerner Publications Company ▪ Minneapolis

Series Editor: Patricia A. Grotts
Series Consultant: Ann L. Burckhardt

Drawings and Map by Jeanette Swofford
Photographs by Robert L. and Diane Wolfe

Additional photographs are reproduced through the courtesy of The Creative Kitchens of Lawry's Foods, Inc. (p. 4) and The Science Museum of Minnesota (p. 11).

The page border for this book is based on an image of an ear of corn carved on an ancient Maya Indian sculpture. The colorful background that appears in the drawings is taken from a traditional painting done on bark paper. In ancient times, Indians in Mexico kept written records on sheets of paper made from the pounded bark of the *amate* tree. Today, people in the state of Guerrero use this same kind of paper for their brightly colored paintings of animals and flowers.

To Mama Coronado, who introduced Mexican food in Minnesota

Library of Congress Cataloging in Publication Data

Coronado, Rosa.
    Cooking the Mexican way.

    (Easy menu ethnic cookbooks)
    Includes index.
    Summary: Introduces fundamentals of Mexican cooking, including special ingredients and cooking utensils. Also provides recipes for suggested dishes.
    1. Cookery, Mexican—Juvenile literature.
2. Mexico—Juvenile literature. [1. Cookery, Mexican. 2. Mexico—Social life and customs] I. Wolfe, Robert L., ill. II. Swofford, Jeanette, ill. III. Title. IV. Series.
TX716.M4C67   641.5972   82-254
ISBN 0-8225-0907-5 (lib. bdg.)

Manufactured in the United States of America

7   8   9   10   11   12   13   14   15   16   99   98   97   96   95   94   93   92   91

CONTENTS

Ensenada

Juárez

Rio Grande

Rio Grande

Sierra Madre Oriental

Grain

Flag of Mexico

Goats

Gulf of California

Sierra Madre Occidental

Beef Cattle

Monterrey

Cows

Cotton

Mazatlán

Pacific Ocean

Tobacco

MEXICO

Tampico

Seafood

Gulf of Mexico

León

Guadalajara

Vegetables

Henequen

Seafood

Mexico City

Sugar Cane

Veracruz

Forest Products

Balsas River

Sierra Madre del Sur

Oaxaca

San Cristóbal

Chocolate

Acapulco

Fruit

Coffee

Pacific Ocean

INTRODUCTION

When North Americans visit Mexico, they often see only the towns just across the border, with their souvenir shops and fast-food stands. These people never get a glimpse of the real Mexico, a large, rich, and complicated country that stretches for a thousand miles beyond the border it shares with its northern neighbor. And they don't get a chance to sample the real goodness of Mexican food.

THE LAND AND THE PEOPLE

The 31 states of Mexico are spread out over a land nearly as varied in climate and geography as the rest of the world put together. Rocky deserts, mountains shrouded in mist, steamy rain forests, fertile plains—all of these can be found in Mexico, often within the same small geographical region.

The lives of the Mexican people are almost as varied as the country's landscape and climate. In the large cities, many Mexicans work in modern office buildings and live in comfortable apartments, while others make their homes in crowded slums. The capital, Mexico City, is the second largest city in the world and has most of the problems that plague big cities everywhere, including traffic jams and air pollution. But outside the capital, there are smaller, less crowded communities like Oaxaca (wah-HAH-kuh), where the air is clean and life is less hectic. In these towns, flowers bloom on the patios of whitewashed houses and young people still take the traditional walk around the central plaza each evening at sunset. And even farther from the bustle of the big city, Indian farmers in the states of Yucatán and Chiapas live in thatch-roofed houses and go to work each day in the corn fields, using the same kinds of tools that their ancestors used a thousand years ago.

A thousand years ago, the country that is now Mexico was inhabited by groups of Maya Indians who had a very advanced civilization. They built large cities out of stone, developed systems of writing and arithmetic, and created beautiful works of art. By the time that soldiers and explorers from Spain arrived in

Mexico during the early 1500s, another powerful group of Indians, the Aztecs, ruled the land from a great city called Tenochtitlán (tay-nosh-tee-TLAHN), located where Mexico City now stands. The Spaniards conquered the Aztecs, destroyed their capital city, and took possession of their land. From this harsh beginning, the modern nation of Mexico was born.

Today most Mexicans are descended from both Spanish and Indian ancestors. They are called *mestizos* (mes-TEEZ-ohs), which means people of mixed blood, and they have inherited the customs and traditions of two very different civilizations. The food of Mexico is a fascinating blend of these two rich traditions.

INDIAN + SPANISH = MEXICAN

The Indians of ancient Mexico ate many foods that were unknown to Europeans in the 1500s, and today these foods are still an important part of the Mexican diet. Among them are corn, tomatoes, squash, avocados, and many varieties of beans and peppers. Another food that ancient Mexicans gave to the world was chocolate, which had a very special meaning to the Aztecs and other Indian civilizations. Chocolate beans were sometimes used as money, and the bitter drink made from them was considered sacred and reserved only for priests and rulers. Chocolate sweetened with sugar is now popular all over the world, but the people of Mexico have a special fondness for it.

Of all the foods native to Mexico, corn is the most popular and most important, today as in the past. The corn tortilla (tor-TEE-yuh), a kind of thin, flat pancake, accompanies almost all Mexican meals, either as a bread or as part of the main dish. A versatile food, the tortilla can be toasted or fried, rolled or folded, stuffed with meats or vegetables, or topped with rich sauces.

Many modern Mexican cooks make their tortillas from a specially prepared dough called *masa* or buy them every day from *tortillerías* (tor-tee-yuh-REE-uhs), stores that sell freshly made tortillas. In some rural areas of the country, however, tortillas are still made in the age-old way. Kernels of dried corn are cooked in lime water until soft and then ground by hand with the *mano* and *metate* (meh-TAH-teh), stone grinding implements used by the Indians of Mexico for centuries. Pieces of the soft corn dough are shaped and flattened by hand until they are just the right thickness and cooked over an open fire on a clay or metal griddle called a *comal*. Tortillas made by this method are delicious, but the process takes a great deal of time. It is not surprising that modern Mexican cooks use shortcuts in preparing this important food.

Another native food essential to Mexican cooking is the chile (CHEE-leh), or pepper. Relatives of the green or bell pepper familiar in North America, Mexican chiles come in many sizes, colors, and flavors. Some are more than 12 inches long, while others are no bigger than a bean. When they are fresh, chiles are usually various shades of green and yellow; when they become ripe, most of them turn bright red or orange. Many chiles have a sweet, mild flavor, but some are so hot that it

makes your eyes water just to smell them. These fabulous peppers have beautiful names like *jalapeño* (hah-la-PEH-nyoh), *poblano* (poh-BLAH-noh), and *serrano* (seh-RRAH-noh), and they are used to give a special flavor to a great variety of Mexican dishes.

Mexican cooking also depends on many ingredients that are not native to the country but were brought from Europe by the early Spanish settlers. Beef, chicken, and pork are European contributions to the Mexican table; the only domestic animals used for food by the Aztecs and other Indians were turkeys and small, fat dogs. Rice and wheat also came from Europe, as did spices like cinnamon and cloves. Because of their European heritage, modern Mexicans enjoy apples and peaches in addition to the papayas, mangoes, and other tropical fruits known to their Indian ancestors.

AT THE MERCADO

When Mexican cooks shop for the fruits, meats, and vegetables needed for the dishes on their menus, they often go to an open-air *mercado* (mer-KAH-doh), or market. Busy markets can be found in the villages and towns of the Mexican countryside as well as in big cities like Guadalajara and Mexico City. Shoppers make a selection from a tempting variety of fruits and vegetables arranged in neat piles in stands or on the ground. There are dark green avocados and bright green limes, golden yellow papayas, rich red tomatoes, and chiles in all shades of green, yellow, and red. In another part of the market are displayed bags full of dried corn and baskets heaped with beans, dark red, pale pink, and spotted like a pinto pony. The air is heavy with the fragrance of ripe fruit and the sharp smell of green herbs like *cilantro* (see-LAHN-troh), or fresh coriander, a popular seasoning. Shoppers quietly bargain over prices and fill their net bags with purchases that will become part of the day's meals.

Markets like these have existed in Mexico for centuries, and they are still an important part of Mexican life. In some large cities, there are *supermercados* (supermarkets) where canned and frozen foods can be obtained, but many Mexican cooks make a daily trip to an out-door market to buy fresh fruits and vegetables. Homes in rural areas of Mexico often have no refrigeration, so food cannot be stored for very long. Even when storage is possible, many Mexican cooks believe that food tastes best when it is prepared fresh every day.

North Americans who want to cook Mexican food usually can't go to an outdoor market and buy fresh chiles. But they can get many of the ingredients they need at local grocery stores and supermarkets. In parts of the United States with large Mexican-American popu-lations, there are stores that sell special ingredients like dried chiles and Mexican chocolate. If you are lucky enough to live in such an area, you can get just about anything you need for a Mexican menu, including stacks of warm, freshly made tortillas. Whether you get your tortillas from a *tortillería* or from the dairy case at the corner supermarket, you should give Mexican cooking a try. The recipes in this book are easy to prepare and will give you a true taste of Mexican food.

An outdoor market in the town of San Cristóbal de las Casas, located in the Mexican state of Chiapas. Every day, Maya Indians who live in this mountainous region come here to buy or sell goods.

BEFORE YOU BEGIN

Cooking any dish, plain or fancy, is easier and more fun if you are familiar with the ingredients. Mexican cooking makes use of some ingredients that you may not know. Sometimes special cookware is used, too, although the recipes in this book can easily be prepared with ordinary utensils and pans.

Before you start cooking, carefully study the following "dictionary" of special ingredients and terms. Then read through the recipe you want to try from beginning to end. Now you are ready to shop for ingredients and to organize the cookware you will need. Once you have assembled everything, you can begin to cook. Before you start, it is also very important to read *The Careful Cook* on page 45. Following these rules will make your cooking experience safe, fun, and easy.

COOKING UTENSILS

fat thermometer — A special thermometer used for testing the temperature of hot fat for frying

molinillo — A special wooden beater with rings of different sizes on it. It can be obtained in shops that specialize in Mexican goods.

tongs — A utensil used to grasp food. Tongs are commonly shaped either like tweezers or scissors, with flat, blunt ends.

To use a *molinillo*, twirl its handle quickly between your palms. The twisting motion of the bottom rings will turn hot chocolate into a creamy drink.

COOKING TERMS

blend—To combine ingredients, usually in a blender, until smooth

boil—To heat a liquid over high heat until bubbles form and rise rapidly to the surface

brown—To cook food quickly in fat over high heat so that the surface turns an even brown

grate—To cut into tiny pieces by rubbing the food against a grater; to shred

knead—To work dough by pressing it with the palms, pushing it outward, and then pressing it over on itself

preheat—To allow an oven to warm up to a certain temperature before putting food in it

sauté—To fry quickly over high heat in oil or fat, stirring or turning the food to prevent burning

shred—To tear or cut into small pieces, either by hand or with a grater

simmer—To cook over low heat in liquid kept just below its boiling point. Bubbles may occasionally rise to the surface.

SPECIAL INGREDIENTS

Mexican food uses some ingredients that may be unfamiliar to you. Among them are such herbs as *basil* (BAYZ-uhl), *oregano* (uh-REHG-uh-noh), and *cumin* (KUHM-un). These rich and fragrant seasonings are the dried leaves and seeds of various kinds of plants. They can be found in the herb and spice sections of most grocery stores. Cumin comes in two forms—whole seeds and a powder made by grinding the seeds. The recipes in this book use only ground cumin.

Another seasoning popular in Mexican food is *garlic,* an herb whose distinctive flavor is also used in Italian and French dishes. Fresh garlic can usually be found in the produce department of a supermarket. Each piece or bulb can be broken up into several small sections called cloves. Most recipes use only one or two finely chopped cloves of this very strong herb. Before you chop up a clove of garlic, you will have to remove the brittle, papery covering that surrounds it.

Most Mexican dishes would be incomplete

Mexican cooking often includes (*clockwise from top*) green or bell peppers, jalapeño chilies, California or Anaheim chilies, serrano chilies, and poblano chilies.

without a few *chiles* for flavor and bite, but these peppers are not widely available in many parts of the United States. Stores that carry Mexican foods will have several kinds of chiles, either fresh or dried. Ordinary supermarkets usually carry two different kinds of canned chiles, spelled "chilies" in English. One is a *green chili,* sometimes called a California green chili. This pepper generally has a mild flavor. The canned *jalapeño chili,* also found in most stores, is much hotter. When cooking with chilies, it is a good idea to add only a small amount at first—even less than the recipe calls for if you are not fond of hot foods. Taste before adding any more. Most cooks rinse canned chilies and take out the seeds before using them.

Two other forms of chilies you will need are *chili powder* and *pimentos.* Chili powder is a mixture of ground chilies and other herbs and spices, including cumin and oregano. Pimentos are small, sweet red chilies that come in cans or bottles and are often used to add color to food. The word is sometimes spelled in the Spanish way—*pimiento.*

Of the many kinds of beans used by Mexican cooks, only two are called for in these recipes, and both are easy to find. One is the large red bean called a *kidney bean* because of its shape. When using canned kidney beans, be sure to drain off the thick liquid and rinse the beans before adding them to your dish. The other bean used here is the dried *pinto bean*— a spotted red bean that has a soft, smooth texture when cooked. This bean is also named for its appearance; *pinto* is the Spanish word for "spotted." Look for pinto beans on the grocery shelf along with other dried beans, peas, and lentils.

When Mexican cooks make pastries or fry foods, they often use *lard*, a solid shortening made from pork fat. In the past, lard was also popular in the United States, but today it is not much used. Some stores have cartons of lard in their dairy departments. If you can't get it, substitute vegetable shortening, butter, margarine, or cooking oil, depending on the recipe.

The beautiful green *avocado*, a fruit native to Mexico, can be found in most parts of the United States. Avocados are ripe when they feel slightly soft to the touch. The ones sold in stores are usually not ripe; you have to take them home and let them sit for a few days before they are ready to use. Other tropical Mexican fruits are not so easy to find. Some stores carry fresh mangoes and papayas, but these fruits do not travel very well. (Of course, if you live in California or Hawaii, you won't have any trouble finding them.) One of the recipes in this book uses canned *mangoes*, which you should be able to find in a large supermarket.

Almost any grocery store will carry *tortillas* in some form. Look for soft, uncooked tortillas in the dairy case. Crisp-fried tortillas for tacos and tostadas are on the shelf with other prepared Mexican foods like taco sauce and enchilada sauce. Packages of tortilla chips can be found with the potato chips.

If you live in an area where there are Mexican stores, you may be able to get fresh, ready-made tortillas just as people in Mexico do. It is also possible to buy a special tortilla flour called *masa harina*, which is mixed with water to make a soft dough. Since shaping the thin, flat tortillas is a real art, however, it might be a good idea to use ready-made tortillas for your first experiments with Mexican food.

A MEXICAN MENU

Below is a simplified menu plan for a typical day of Mexican cooking. The Spanish names of the dishes are given, along with a guide on how to pronounce them. Two alternate dinner and supper ideas are included. Recipes for the starred items can be found in this book.

ENGLISH	ESPAÑOL	PRONUNCIATION GUIDE
MENU	EL MENÚ	el meh-NOO
Breakfast	*El Desayuno*	el deh-sey-YOO-noh
*Mexican hot chocolate	Chocolate Mexicano	choh-koh-LAH-teh meh-he-KAH-noh
Sweet rolls	Pan dulce	pahn DOOL-seh
Dinner	*La Comida*	la koh-MEE-duh
I	I	
*Vermicelli soup	Sopa de fideos	SOH-pah deh fee-DAY-ohs
*Tortillas with chicken	Enchiladas con pollo	ehn-cheh-LAH-dahs kohn POY-yoh
*Refried beans	Frijoles refritos	free-HOH-less rreh-FREE-tohs
*Mango with cinnamon	Mango canela	MAHN-goh kah-NAY-lah
II	II	
*Avocado dip	Guacamole	gwah-kah-MOH-leh
*Mexican rice	Arroz Mexicano	ah-RROS meh-he-KAH-noh
*Red snapper with lime juice	Huachinango con jugos	hwa-chee-NAHN-goh kohn HOO-gohs
or *Hamburger hash	de limas o Picadillo	deh LEEM-ahs oh pee-kah-DEE-yoh
*Zucchini and corn	Calabacitas y elote	kah-lah-bah-SEE-tahs ee eh-LOH-teh
Fresh fruit	Frutas frescas	FROO-tahs FREHS-kahs

ENGLISH	ESPAÑOL	PRONUNCIATION GUIDE
Snacks	**Botanas**	boh-TAHN-ahs
*Tacos	Tacos	TAH-kohs
*Tomato sauce	Salsa cruda	SAHL-suh KROOD-uh
*Fried pastry	Buñuelos	boo-NYUE-lohs
*Fried tortillas with cheese	Nachos	NAH-chohs
Supper	**La Cena**	lah SEH-nuh
I	I	
*Kidney bean salad	Ensalada de frijoles	en-sah-LAH-dah deh free-HOH-less
Hot tortillas	Tortillas calientes	tor-TEE-yahs kahl-ee-EN-tehs
*Rice with milk	Arroz con leche	ah-RROS kohn LEH-cheh
II	II	
*Crisp tortillas with beef	Tostadas con carne	toh-STAH-dahs kohn KAR-nay
Lemonade	Limonada	lee-mohn-AH-dah

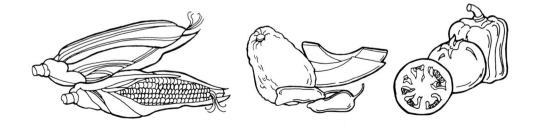

BREAKFAST/
El Desayuno

Rural and urban Mexicans differ in their breakfast-eating habits. Country people rise very early so they can work in the fields. When they first get up at about 5 A.M., they might have a sweet roll and either *cafe con leche* (coffee mixed with hot milk), hot chocolate, or a hot cornmeal drink called *atole* (ah-TOH-lay). City people eat a similar meal, but between 7 and 9 A.M. In the country, 9 A.M. is the time for a second breakfast, which is much more hearty than the first. Fruit or fruit juice, eggs, beans, chili sauce, tortillas, and *cafe con leche* may be served. This meal is called *almuerzo* (ahl-MUER-soh). Those people in the city who have only breakfasted on a cup of coffee are also likely to eat *almuerzo,* but again they eat it much later than the country people. A city *almuerzo* is a meal eaten closer to the time of a North American lunch, at 11 or 11:30 A.M. Because people in Mexico don't like eating early, however, this meal is not called an early lunch but rather a late breakfast.

Hot chocolate flavored with cinnamon is a favorite breakfast beverage in Mexico.

Mexican Hot Chocolate/ Chocolate Mexicano

Stores that sell Mexican foods usually carry a special form of chocolate used to make this delicious chocolate drink. It comes in cakes or tablets and contains sugar and cinnamon. If you can't get this special chocolate, sweet cooking chocolate can be used instead.

In Mexico, hot chocolate is customarily served in a large earthenware jug. It is placed on the table, where the chocolate is whipped into a froth with a wooden beater called a molinillo *(moh-lee-NEE-yoh). The drawing on page 12 shows how a* molinillo *is used. If you can't find one in your neighborhood, a hand eggbeater will work just as well.*

2 3-ounce cakes or tablets of Mexican chocolate or 6 ounces of sweet cooking chocolate
6 cups milk
1½ teaspoons cinnamon (if using cooking chocolate)

1. Combine all ingredients in a saucepan and cook over low heat. Stir constantly until chocolate has melted and mixture is blended.
2. With a *molinillo* or eggbeater, beat chocolate to a froth just before serving.

Serves 4

DINNER/La Comida

Mexicans in both the city and the country generally eat their main meal in the middle of the day, sometime between 2 and 5:30 P.M. Rural people usually eat a stew, beans, and tortillas. Wealthier people in the city may have four or five courses: soup, rice or noodles, a main course of meat or fish, vegetable, and dessert.

The tradition of eating a big meal in the afternoon is part of Mexico's Spanish heritage. Mexicans say it is also a habit that promotes good health. People who live in the mountainous areas of Mexico believe that the high altitude tends to slow down digestion. In 7,600-foot-high Mexico City, it makes sense to eat a big meal in the afternoon rather than in the evening before bedtime. But today the customs of modern life are beginning to interfere with this traditional eating habit. Mexicans who work in offices and factories often don't have time for a big meal during the day. So they eat a light lunch at noon like working people in other parts of the modern world.

Vermicelli Soup/ Sopa de Fideos

Fideos is the Spanish name for vermicelli, thin noodles often used in Italian cooking.

½ **cup vermicelli noodles, uncooked and broken into small pieces**
1 **tablespoon bacon fat or vegetable oil**
½ **cup finely chopped onion**
3 **tablespoons tomato puree**
2½ **15-ounce cans (about 5 cups) beef broth**
½ **cup grated Monterey Jack or white cheddar cheese**

1. Heat fat or oil in a skillet. Add noodles, fry until light brown, and remove.
2. In same fat, sauté onions until they are soft. Add tomato puree and cook for 2 to 3 minutes, stirring constantly.
3. Simmer puree, noodles, and broth in a large pan until noodles are tender (6 to 8 minutes). Add salt and pepper to taste.
4. Sprinkle with cheese and serve.

Serves 4

Sopa de fideos is easy to fix and makes a good beginning for a meal.

Tortillas with Chicken/ Enchiladas con Pollo

Enchiladas *are one of the most versatile foods on the Mexican menu. These filled and rolled tortillas can be made in many different ways. The filling can be meat, cheese, vegetables, or any combination of these ingredients. You can top* enchiladas *with a canned tomato-and-chili sauce, or you can make your own sauce out of red or green tomatoes.*

The recipe given here is for enchiladas *filled with chicken and cheese, plus a few other good things. The basic directions for preparing and cooking the tortillas can be used with any filling, so why not try some other combinations. How about browned ground beef and refried beans? Or hard-cooked eggs and* guacamole?

Basic enchilada recipe:

8 7-inch corn tortillas
2 tablespoons vegetable oil
  heated sauce
  filling
  sour cream

1. Heat oil in a skillet and fry tortilla for only a few seconds. (Tortilla should be limp and soft.)
2. Remove tortilla with tongs and dip in heated sauce, making sure it is well coated.
3. Place tortilla on a cutting board and put about ¼ cup filling in the center. Roll up and put in a baking pan with the opening face down.
4. When all tortillas have been fried, filled, and placed in the pan, cover them with remaining sauce. Cook in a 350° oven until sauce is bubbly (about 15 or 20 minutes).
5. Serve each enchilada with a spoonful of cold sour cream.

Serves 4

Chicken and cheese filling:

2 large chicken breasts
2 teaspoons vegetable oil
1 large onion, chopped
1 large green pepper, cleaned out and chopped
½ teaspoon oregano
½ teaspoon basil
10 ounces Monterey Jack cheese, grated (2½ cups when grated)

1. Simmer chicken breasts in 3 cups water until tender (about 25 to 30 minutes).
2. While chicken cooks, heat oil in a frying pan. Sauté onion, green pepper, oregano, and basil until onion and pepper are soft.
3. Drain chicken. When it has cooled enough to handle, remove bones and slice each breast into 6 strips.
4. Place chicken strip in center of fried tortilla that has been dipped in sauce. Spoon on about 2 tablespoons each of onion-pepper mixture and cheese. Roll up.
5. Pour on sauce and cook according to basic directions.

Makes filling for 8 tortillas

Enchilada sauce:

To top your enchiladas, use 3 10-ounce cans of enchilada sauce (mild or hot), heated. If you would like to make your own enchilada sauce, here is a simple recipe using chili powder.

1 medium-sized onion, finely chopped
2 tablespoons vegetable oil
3½ cups tomato puree
2 cloves garlic, finely chopped
4 tablespoons chili powder
½ teaspoon ground cumin
¼ teaspoon oregano
1 teaspoon salt

1. Sauté onion in oil until it is soft and yellow. Add tomato puree and garlic.
2. Gradually stir in chili powder, cumin, oregano, and salt.
3. Cover and simmer about 30 minutes, stirring frequently.

Makes about 3 cups

Refried Beans/
Frijoles Refritos

Refried beans are served at almost every meal in Mexico. The beans are not really fried twice, as the name suggests, but they are usually cooked or heated twice. Mexicans often make large batches of beans and then reheat them during the week as needed, adding a little more lard each time.

2 cups dried pinto beans
5 cups water
1 large onion, chopped
2 teaspoons vegetable oil
½ cup lard, butter, or bacon fat
1 teaspoon salt

1. Wash beans thoroughly under cold running water. Put beans in a pan containing 10 cups water and soak them for 6 to 8 hours.
2. Rinse beans and place them in a large kettle with 5 cups water, onion, and oil.
3. Cook over high heat for 1 hour or until beans are soft.
4. Add lard and salt and mash with a potato masher until all fat has melted.
5. Lower heat and continue to cook beans, stirring occasionally, for about 2½ hours or until bean mixture is thick and heavy.

Serves 8

Serve refried beans as a side dish or use them as a filling for tacos and enchiladas.

Mango with Cinnamon/
Mango Canela

Mango canela *is a spicy and cooling treat.*

1-pound can mangoes
¼ cup shredded coconut
1 teaspoon cinnamon

1. Chill can of mangoes overnight in the refrigerator.
2. To serve, place each mango section in a dessert dish or fruit cup, top with coconut, and sprinkle lightly with cinnamon.

Serves 4 to 6

Blairsville Junior High Library
Blairsville, PA 15717

Guacamole and raw vegetables are perfect summertime eating.

Avocado Dip/
Guacamole

In the United States, this avocado mixture is usually served as a dip, but in Mexico it has many other uses. Guacamole makes a good topping for tacos or tostadas and a refreshing salad all by itself.

There are many ways to make this popular food, and all of them are delicious. The essential ingredients are avocados and lime or lemon juice. Without the fruit juice, the avocados quickly turn brown, so be sure to add it.

How many chilies you use depends on how hot you want your guacamole. *Taste it before adding too many. Instead of chilies, you can use a dash of chili powder or Tabasco sauce for a little heat.*

2 large (or 4 small) ripe avocados
1 small tomato, chopped
½ small onion, chopped
1 to 3 canned green chilies, chopped
1 tablespoon lime or lemon juice
¾ teaspoon salt
pepper to taste

1. Cut avocados in half lengthwise. Pry out pits with the point of a knife. Peel and cut into small pieces. (If avocados are very ripe, you can scoop the flesh out of the shells with a spoon.)
2. Mash avocados with a fork and blend in other ingredients. For a very smooth mixture, combine ingredients in a blender.
3. Serve with tortilla chips or raw vegetables.

Makes about 2 cups

Red tomatoes and green peppers make *arroz Mexicano* a colorful and delicious *sopa seca*.

Mexican Rice/
Arroz Mexicano

Mexican rice belongs to an unusual category of Mexican dishes called dry soups—sopas secas. To make a sopa seca, a starchy food such as rice, noodles, or cut-up tortillas is cooked slowly in a soup broth. Eventually the broth is completely absorbed by the starch, leaving a "dry" soup. Dry soups are served as a separate course before the meat course.

  1 cup white rice, uncooked
  2 tablespoons vegetable oil
  4 cups tomato juice
  4 tablespoons butter or margarine
  ½ teaspoon ground cumin
  1 teaspoon salt
  ½ green pepper, cleaned out and
      chopped
  2 garlic cloves, finely chopped
1½ cups chopped onion
  2 large tomatoes, chopped, or 1
      8-ounce can (1 cup) tomatoes,
      cut up with a spoon

1. Rinse and drain rice. Dry on paper towels.
2. In a large frying pan, heat oil and fry raw rice until it becomes brown.
3. In a saucepan, heat tomato juice. Add to rice in the frying pan.
4. Add rest of ingredients, cover, and cook over low heat until tomato juice is absorbed and rice is soft (about 20 minutes).

Serves 4 to 6

Serve red snapper fillets with lime wedges for a light, nutritious lunch or dinner.

Red Snapper with Lime Juice/ Huachinango con Jugos de Limas

Huachinango is an Aztec name for red snapper, an ocean fish caught off the shores of tropical Veracruz, a Mexican state located on the Gulf of Mexico. If you visit the fish market in the busy seaport of Veracruz, you will see stands full of freshly caught red snapper with shining scales in all shades of red, pink, and yellow. This fish is also available fresh or frozen in many parts of the United States.

There are many popular Mexican recipes using red snapper, but one of the tastiest ways to fix this fish is simply to pan fry it and then squeeze on fresh lime juice. Limes are more widely used in Mexican cooking than lemons. Their sweet, tangy juice gives a special flavor to fish and to fresh fruits like papaya and mango.

6 red snapper fillets
½ cup all-purpose flour seasoned with salt and pepper
4 tablespoons vegetable oil
2 limes, cut into wedges

1. Dust fillets lightly with mixture of flour, salt, and pepper.
2. Heat oil in a skillet and sauté fillets for about 5 minutes or until they are golden brown. Turn and sauté on other side.
3. Serve with lime wedges.

Serves 6

Hamburger Hash/
Picadillo

1 pound lean ground beef
1 small onion, finely chopped
⅛ teaspoon garlic salt
⅛ teaspoon ground cumin
   salt to taste
2 large tomatoes, cut into wedges
1 canned green chili, chopped
   (optional)
3 tablespoons raisins
2 teaspoons slivered almonds
4 sprigs fresh parsley

1. Simmer ground beef and onion in a frying pan over medium heat. Stir often, breaking up beef gently.
2. Add garlic salt, cumin, and salt.
3. When beef is nearly all browned and cooked through, drain fat from the pan. Then add tomatoes, chili, raisins, and almonds. Continue to simmer for another 2 minutes.
4. Garnish each serving with parsley.

Serves 4

Zucchini and Corn/
Calabacitas y Elote

3 medium-sized zucchini
½ cup canned or frozen corn, cooked
   salt to taste
   pepper to taste
1 small tomato, cut into quarters
¼ cup grated cheddar cheese

1. Wash zucchini and cut into ½-inch cubes.
2. Place zucchini in a saucepan with corn, salt, pepper, and tomato.
3. Cover the saucepan and simmer about 8 minutes or until zucchini is tender. (Do not add any water. Juices of zucchini and tomato will provide enough liquid for cooking.)
4. Top with grated cheese.

Serves 4

For a change of pace, use *picadillo* for a sandwich filling and serve zucchini and corn as a vegetarian main dish.

SNACKS/Botanas

Tacos

The word "taco" actually means "snack" in Spanish, but today this word is used for one dish in particular. A taco is a sandwich type of snack made with tortillas, a meat or bean filling, garnish, and spicy sauce. Tortillas that have already been folded and fried are often called "taco shells" and are available at most supermarkets. If you would like to make your own shells, read the recipe below.

6 7-inch corn tortillas
½ cup vegetable oil
1¼ cups precooked, shredded or
ground meat such as beef, pork,
or chicken, or refried beans
(see recipe on page 24)
shredded lettuce, chopped
tomatoes, and grated cheddar
cheese for garnish
bottled taco sauce or homemade
salsa cruda

1. Preheat ½ cup oil in a frying pan.
2. Place tortilla in oil and fry lightly on one side. Turn over and fold in half with tongs. Then fry both sides of folded tortilla to desired crispness.
3. Drain on a paper towel. Fry each tortilla in the same way and drain.
4. Fill folded taco shells with meat or beans and desired condiments. (Use about 3 tablespoons of filling for each taco.) Pass sauce so that everyone can help themselves. (Green and red pepper, pimento, onion, and kidney beans are delicious additions to any kind of taco.)

Serves 6

Tomato Sauce/
Salsa Cruda

If you would like to have a homemade sauce for your tacos, try this simple one made of fresh tomatoes and green chilies. Called salsa cruda *(fresh or raw sauce), this spicy mixture can usually be found on all Mexican tables right next to the salt and pepper. It makes a good addition to almost any Mexican dish.*

**6 medium-sized tomatoes, finely
    chopped
½ cup (more or less to taste) finely
    chopped canned green chilies
⅓ cup finely chopped onion
1 teaspoon salt**

Mix all ingredients together in a bowl. (If you want a little more fire in your *salsa,* add a finely chopped *jalapeño* chili.)
Makes about 3 cups

Fried Pastry/
Buñuelos

This pastry is popular all over Mexico, but it is a special favorite in the state of Oaxaca, located in the south-central part of the country. The people of Oaxaca eat buñuelos *during the Christmas season, and there is an interesting custom associated with the pastries. On Christmas Eve, street vendors sell* buñuelos *in the town plazas, handing them to customers on pottery dishes that have cracks or flaws in them. After eating the pastries, the people throw the dishes on the ground and break them. This custom seems to have very ancient roots and may be connected to old Indian ceremonies celebrating the end of the old year and the beginning of a new one.*

If you are ever in Oaxaca on Christmas Eve, you can join the local people in eating buñuelos *and smashing dishes. With the help of this recipe, you can also enjoy the delicious pastry in your own home.*

4 cups all-purpose flour
2 tablespoons sugar
1 tablespoon baking powder
2 eggs
2 tablespoons milk
¼ cup vegetable oil
1 cup warm water
1 cup vegetable oil (for frying)
½ cup sugar
3 tablespoons cinnamon

1. Thoroughly mix flour, sugar, and baking powder in a large bowl.
2. In another bowl, beat together eggs and milk. Then add to dry ingredients. Stir in ¼ cup oil and mix well.
3. Add warm water and mix until dough can be handled easily. (If dough is too dry, add a few more teaspoons warm water, one at a time.)
4. Place dough on a lightly floured board and knead until smooth.
5. Divide dough into 20 to 24 pieces and shape each into a ball. Flatten balls on the board with the palm of your hand. Cover with a cloth for 20 minutes.

6. On a lightly floured board, roll out each flattened ball with a rolling pin into a large round shape about 6 or 7 inches in diameter. Let stand for about 5 minutes.

7. Heat 1 cup oil in an electric frying pan set at 360°. (If you don't have an electric frying pan, use a fat thermometer to check the temperature of oil heated in a regular frying pan.) Just before frying, stretch each *buñuelo* a little more by hand.

8. Fry each *buñuelo* until underside is golden brown (about 3 minutes). Turn and fry other side until crisp. Remove and drain on a paper towel.

9. In a small bowl, combine sugar and cinnamon. Sprinkle hot *buñuelos* with cinnamon and sugar mixture.

Makes 20 to 24

1. Flatten ball of dough with your palms. 2. Roll flattened ball into a 6- or 7-inch circle. 3. Gently stretch dough before frying. 4. Fry dough until golden brown on each side.

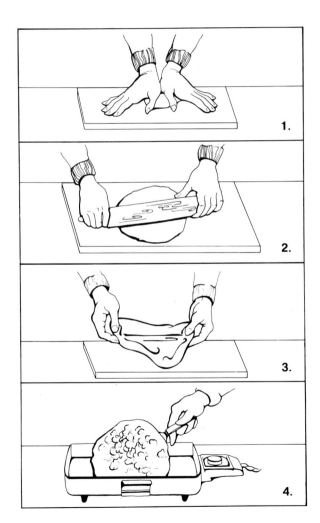

Hot *buñuelos* dusted with cinnamon and sugar are a treat for any special occasion.

Fried Tortillas with Cheese/Nachos

Nachos *are crisp, tasty snacks made out of fried corn tortillas.*

2 7-inch corn tortillas
½ cup vegetable oil
4 ounces cheddar cheese, grated
   (1 cup when grated)
1 green pepper, cleaned out and cut
   into strips

1. Cut each tortilla into 6 to 8 triangles.
2. Heat oil in a frying pan. Drop in tortilla sections and fry until golden brown.
3. Using tongs, remove sections and drain on a paper towel. Let cool.
4. Preheat the oven to 250°.
5. When fried tortillas are cool, place them on a cookie sheet and sprinkle with grated cheese. Garnish each piece with strip of green pepper.
6. Bake until cheese is melted (about 5 or 10 minutes).

Serves 6 to 8

SUPPER/
La Cena

Traditionally, Mexicans eat a very light meal at night. The everyday evening meal, called the *merienda,* is served in the early evening, around 6 or 7 P.M. At this meal, many Mexicans have only *cafe con leche* or hot chocolate and sweet rolls. Sometimes the *merienda* is more like the kind of meal served at teatime in England. On these occasions, people might eat tortillas, beans, or perhaps some cold meat in addition to coffee and hot chocolate.

A more formal supper served later in the evening is called the *cena.* It is still a light meal but more special than the *merienda.* Mexicans might have this kind of a meal when guests are invited or when there is a birthday to celebrate. The *cena* is eaten anytime after 8 P.M. and often as late as midnight.

Kidney Bean Salad/
Ensalada de Frijoles

- **3 tablespoons olive or vegetable oil**
- **1½ tablespoons vinegar**
- **1 garlic clove, finely chopped**
- **⅛ teaspoon chili powder**
- **½ teaspoon oregano**
- **1 16-ounce can (2 cups) kidney beans, drained**
- **1 green pepper, cleaned out and chopped**
- **½ cup chopped red onion**
- **1 tablespoon chopped pimento**
- **12 pitted black olives, sliced**
- **½ head lettuce**

1. Put oil, vinegar, garlic, chili powder, and oregano in a small jar with a tight lid. Shake vigorously.
2. In a large bowl, mix other ingredients (except lettuce) with oil mixture.
3. Chill 2 hours or more in the refrigerator.
4. Arrange lettuce leaves on a plate and spoon salad on top.

Serves 4

Ensalada de frijoles is a colorful side dish.

Delicious *tostadas* are as fun to make as they are to eat. Be sure to use a fork or spoon to scoop up every last bite!

Crisp Tortillas with Beef/ Tostadas con Carne

For a variation of this recipe, replace the beef with sliced pork, chicken, or shrimp.

½ cup vegetable oil
12 7-inch corn tortillas
1 pound ground beef
½ cup chopped onion
1 10-ounce can green chilies and
    tomatoes
½ teaspoon garlic salt
½ teaspoon oregano
½ teaspoon ground cumin
¼ teaspoon chili powder
¼ teaspoon basil
1 15-ounce can (about 2 cups)
    refried beans or 2 cups home-
    made refried beans (see recipe
    on page 24)
2 cups shredded lettuce
2 tomatoes, chopped or sliced
4 ounces cheddar cheese, grated
    (1 cup when grated)
    taco sauce or *salsa cruda*

1. Heat oil in a frying pan. Using tongs, submerge tortillas, one or two at a time, in hot oil and fry until each is crisp. Drain on a paper towel and stack.
2. Cook beef and onion in a skillet until meat is brown.
3. Drain off excess fat from meat and onions. Stir in chilies-tomato mixture, garlic salt, oregano, cumin, chili powder, and basil.
4. Simmer, uncovered, for 15 minutes.
5. Heat refried beans.
6. Spread each tortilla with warm beans and then cover beans with 2 heaping tablespoons of meat mixture.
7. Top with lettuce, tomato, and cheese. Pour on taco sauce or *salsa cruda* to taste.

Serves 6

Rice with Milk/
Arroz con Leche

This rice pudding is quite sweet, which is just the way Mexicans like it. If you prefer less sweetness, use ½ cup condensed milk with ½ cup regular milk.

½ **cup white rice, uncooked**
½ **cinnamon stick**
1½ **cups water**
1 **cup sweetened condensed milk**
2½ **tablespoons raisins**
   cinnamon for garnish

1. Put rice, cinnamon stick, and water in a saucepan. Bring to a boil quickly. Reduce heat, cover, and simmer until water is absorbed (about 15 to 20 minutes).
2. Add milk and raisins. Cook, uncovered, until milk works into rice (10 to 15 minutes).
3. Remove from heat, take out cinnamon stick, and cover. Let sit for a few minutes. Sprinkle with cinnamon.
4. Serve rice hot or cold.

Serves 4

Arroz con leche is a sweet, raisin-studded dessert spiced with cinnamon.

THE CAREFUL COOK

Whenever you cook, there are certain safety rules you must always keep in mind. Even experienced cooks follow these rules when they are in the kitchen.

1. Always wash your hands before handling food.
2. Thoroughly wash all raw vegetables and fruits to remove dirt, chemicals, and insecticides.
3. Use a cutting board when cutting up vegetables and fruits. Don't cut them up in your hand! And be sure to cut in a direction *away* from you and your fingers.
4. Long hair or loose clothing can easily catch fire if brought near the burners of a stove. If you have long hair, tie it back before you start cooking.
5. Turn all pot handles toward the back of the stove so that you will not catch your sleeve or jewelry on them. This is especially important when younger brothers and sisters are around. They could easily knock off a pot and get burned.

6. Always use a pot holder to steady hot pots or to take pans out of the oven. Don't use a wet cloth on a hot pan because the steam it produces could burn you.
7. Lift the lid of a steaming pot with the opening away from you so that you will not get burned.
8. If you get burned, hold the burn under cold running water. Do not put grease or butter on it. Cold water helps to take the heat out, but grease or butter will only keep it in.
9. If grease or cooking oil catches fire, throw baking soda or salt at the bottom of the flame to put it out. (Water will *not* put out a grease fire.) Call for help and try to turn all the stove burners to "off."

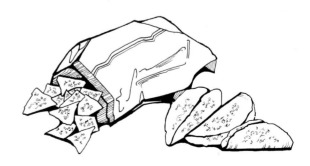

METRIC CONVERSION CHART

WHEN YOU KNOW	MULTIPLY BY	TO FIND
MASS (weight)		
ounces (oz)	28.0	grams (g)
pounds (lb)	0.45	kilograms (kg)
VOLUME		
teaspoons (tsp)	5.0	milliliters (ml)
tablespoons (Tbsp)	15.0	milliliters
fluid ounces (oz)	30.0	milliliters
cup (c)	0.24	liters (l)
pint (pt)	0.47	liters
quart (qt)	0.95	liters
gallon (gal)	3.8	liters
TEMPERATURE		
Fahrenheit (°F) temperature	5/9 (after subtracting 32)	Celsius (°C) temperature

COMMON MEASURES AND THEIR EQUIVALENTS

3 teaspoons = 1 tablespoon

8 tablespoons = ½ cup

2 cups = 1 pint

2 pints = 1 quart

4 quarts = 1 gallon

16 ounces = 1 pound

INDEX

ABOUT THE AUTHOR

Rosa Coronado began learning about Mexican cooking when she was very young. Her parents, Don Arturo and Dona Elvira Coronado, wanted their daughter to grow up knowing as much as possible about her Mexican heritage. When the Coronados opened La Casa Coronado in Minneapolis, Minnesota, 7-year-old Rosa helped her mother in the restaurant by cleaning chili pods and operating the tortilla machine. When she was 15, Rosa catered a Christmas dinner all by herself.

After graduating from high school, Coronado attended the University of Mexico in Mexico City. Since that time, she has been involved in the food industry as a restauranteur and a cooking school instructor. Coronado also lectures to many groups about Mexican history and culture. In 1975, Coronado became the first woman admitted to the Geneva Executive Chefs Association, an international organization of chefs and food specialists.